My Transformation Journal

BELONGS TO

....

....

....

....

....

Front cover and all illustrations by Melissa Halliday.
Photos by Melissa Halliday.

Remember your Bliss & Abundance and Breathe!

About the Author

Melissa Halliday is a yoga teacher, Marriage & Funeral celebrant, singer, Picaluna Funeral Director, facilitator of Death Café Newtown, Death Midwife & Facilitator of the '10 Things to Know before you Go' Workshop (www.thegroundswellproject.com)

Human mother to Chaska, Fur Baby Mama to Mahika the japalier & Turtle Mama to Lulu & Truffle.

She is a flawed, fabulous human being just like you. Yoga and meditation, pilates, singing, watercolour painting & travel (even if just out to the garden!) are all integral to her body/mind sanity toolkit. She is doing her best to make sense of this world and her place in it whilst trying to avoid accidental run ins with chocolate bars and Tim Tams. She lives in Sydney, Australia and is passionate about death literacy: starting end of life conversations that allow others to feel more comfortable talking about death, find more meaning in the lives they have left to live and take action for themselves and their families to do death differently. She is inspired by nature, music and spiritual seekers on every path and looks forward to walking the Larapinta Trail, travelling further in Australia before heading back one day to Cuba, Turkey, India & Luang Prabang in Laos.

Dedication: To my beautiful daughter Chaska (meaning little star of love) You are loved beyond knowing, appreciated beyond understanding. Shine bright beyond galaxies. Lean in to your uniqueness and magnificence. Inspire others to transform fear into love, resistance into flow & acceptance, challenges into opportunities for greater awareness, growth, resilience & compassion. Follow your star on both your journey and destination of peace and love in your heart of hearts.

To All Souls:

My wish for you on your path to greater peace, truth, happiness, wisdom and transformation:

May all beings be healthy, happy, safe,
peaceful in their heart of hearts
& free from suffering.

The artist Pablo Picasso said *"The meaning of life is to find your gift. The purpose of life is to give it away."*

May this Journal help you clarify your abundant gifts so you can better express & share them to the world...

Welcome beautiful soul!

I searched high and low for a simple, beautiful journal that was easy to use and could track the changes I wanted to make in my life on a daily basis. Nothing gave me a simple focus on the issues that, as a woman, were close to my heart, delivered in a format I loved to use to track my emotional & spiritual progress. SO I created this journal to motivate myself, and lift myself up after heartbreak, low self confidence and a need for more motivation to get through a tough phase in my life. Journals are like good friends that listen without judgement and support you through the best and worst of life.

You don't need to be in a tough place to benefit from journaling and being your own compassionate therapist of the spirit and emotions, whatever your gender. As we look back on our progress and clarify our purpose, we identify blocks in understanding and carve a new path forward more aligned to our heartfelt goals and the gifts we wish to express in the world.

Do any of these apply to you?

Some days I feel so strong and powerful but others are a shit sandwich!

I am confused about what to do with my life or the next direction I want to take.

I deserve to love myself, see my worth and know I'm enough but loving myself doesn't come easy at times.

I want to value and respect myself more and have my own back, focus on abundance and gratitude for what I have and put healthy boundaries in place so people value and respect me.

When I worry or obsess about the past and things that are gone that I can't change, it blocks my opportunities to live a contented present and manifest a happier future.

I contribute to the happiness, wealth and prosperity of others but how do I grow my own?

I know I am a result of the thoughts I choose to think, the food I put in my precious body and the problems I try to avoid that keep recurring in my life: it's my choice to think, eat and live better in a way that works for me.

I need motivation on a daily basis to push through the challenges and live my best life, to remind me I am enough, set up healthier patterns, clearer focus & to help me ease into my day.

Well you asked for it. A simple, inspiring journal to track progress as you move through life:days and daily ways to speak your truth and become your own loving & supportive therapist!

Journaling is a delicious way to pour yourself onto a page with no judgement, just pure acceptance of what is. This is how I feel and where I am today; this is what I need to release that is holding me back in love, career, finance, relationships. This is what I am grateful for and which gives me the energy to move forward to the things I want to manifest.

We can all talk the talk but how often do we lean in and walk the talk? Act in alignment with our greatest desires? Work out what is holding us back and what we want to release? Give ourselves permission and space to relax, be creative, imaginative and remember to practise gratitude; help us persist through the resistance and do life on our terms? Motivate us to give to ourselves the very things we so freely give to others: friendship, loyalty, generosity, joy, peace, support, inspiration?

So, let's shine the light back on ourselves and give ourselves the freedom to do life on our own terms without having to please others! This is a permission to think, dream and create big and be as selfish as we like with it, kind of journal!

When we fill our own tank first, and nourish our spirit, we have more in reserve to give to the relationships and things that are important to us.

It's time!

This is not a job we can delegate. We are the only ones who can do this inner work.

So, this Journal is designed to set you up for a day of focus, freedom, truth and empowerment that only you can give yourself.

The idea is simple. Attention plus intention creates magic, miracles and manifestation in our life. Get clear on your focus and intention, the why and what you want. Sprinkle on some gratitude and inspiration and leave the timing, the how and when, to the Universe and Spirit to sort out.

The Process is simple: Around 5 mins

1 **Dream**: Write down any dreams at the bottom of the page when you wake up and get those out first. You can analyse them later.
2 **Feeling**: Identify a feeling/s that come up at the top of the page as you sit to write.
3 **Release**: What it is that feels stuck that you may need to release to be more free?
4 Is there any **healing** you need to tap into. If you feel sad focus on things that will bring in more joy; if you feel angry, negative or resentful- try the H'opono'pono prayer below or do a guided meditation (see below) or some yoga to ground and soothe yourself.
5 **Gratitude**: Connect in with what you are grateful for today; the air we breathe, the birds that sing, the friendships that nourish us, the opportunities to help others.
6 Think of the things that **inspire and energise you**. Music, hobbies, conversations, relationships, anything at all!
7 **Create a focus for the day** and decide what qualities you will bring to your day to attract, resonate with and amplify that focus e.g. being generous and giving of time, attention, resources to others if you want people to be generous towards you. **Be the qualities you wish to attract** – they

may include kindness, patience, focused action, clarity, balance, love, acceptance, understanding, resilience..... then let go and let God (Source, the Divine, Higher Power) get to work on your behalf.....

Dreams

Dreams are personal but they are also archetypal and can reveal information and sometimes solutions to what our conscious mind may have been troubling over. Archetypes are condensed, symbolic representations of ideas, stories and qualities understood across any divides of language and culture which speak to common themes of the human condition such as love, pain, power, conflict, insecurities etc. Dreams can carry a lot of messages from our subconscious. Trust your intuition as it will give you clues on how to interpret your dreams.

I have had dreams such as feeling trapped in a house where I had to look behind different doors (the choices in my life at the time that felt overwhelming), dreams where my feet would not move at a time when I felt stuck and unable to move in my life: dreams where I was on a life raft or at a party surrounded by people yet feeling incredibly lonely or disconnected from the others in the dream- all messages from the deeper levels of mind that it was time to make some changes in my life.... so don't let dreams scare you. It's always better that the scary stuff plays out in dreams so you don't have to go through it in real life!

Just reflect on what they mean to you or look up the symbols in a Dream book or check online. Trust that the meaning you give them is your intuition telling you the message you need to hear. If you have trouble remembering dreams, just set an alarm clock for early in the morning around the full moon when our subconscious can be more active and tell yourself as you go to sleep 'tonight I intend to remember my dreams'. Have your Journal nearby with a pen to jot down any dreams when you wake.

Tarot as an Example of Archetypes that may help interpret our dreams

In the tarot, the cards carry powerful, universally understood archetypes. For example, the Empress is the symbol of the Divine Feminine- creative, abundant, wise, intuitive; sometimes she is interpreted as the pregnant, fertile mother. Her image contains depths of meaning understood across the world, in whatever language.

Each tarot deck has major arcana cards like the Sun (happiness, confidence, strength, joy), the Fool (new beginnings/a leap of faith), the Tower card (shock or surprise you didn't see coming). It also has minor arcana cards divided into four categories: Cups, Swords, Wands and Pentacles (from the Ace through to the King and Queen).

The Cups represent water: the emotions, love and relationships; the Swords represent air: ideas, intellect, reason, defence, conflict, discernment and cutting away old ideas, people and things that don't serve us; the Pentacles represent earth: the material plane, work, possessions, things of value; the Wands represent passion, quick movement, sexuality etc.

A good tarot reader can interpret the archetypes and the story the cards are conveying through their meanings. The placement of the cards in the spread can also alter their meanings in the context of the story, as can reversals of the cards. I recommend getting the original basic Rider Waite tarot deck if you want to dig deeper into the tarot & these wonderful archetypes.

Like the tarot, the stories we have in our dreams can provide clues to what is causing us anxiety or joy in our lives as well as solutions to our problems. Some dreams are so busy that we may just see them as the subconscious' way of releasing the clutter that we have collected from the movies and Netflix bingeing we have been doing! Like a pressure cooker, our thoughts need an escape valve and dreams can be a way of letting go of the mental anxiety and excess baggage.

Release

What stands in the way of you having the peace, freedom, love, health and abundance you desire? Is it time to let go of anxiety, despair, not-enoughness, guilt or fears that keep you stuck, small and not performing, feeling, thinking or being your optimal version of you?

Our caveman programming is hardwired into our brains and instinct can still perceive threats and set us up for fight, flight or freeze/stagnation responses that can override our conscious mind that knows we are safe from marauding dinosaurs, falling ladders, worst case scenarios that usually never happen. Who during Covid didn't feel that negative spiral of thoughts overwhelming us at times? It's called catastrophising. We can all do it when we are feeling Hungry, Angry, Lonely or Tired H.A.L.T. Then we know it's time to stop and take stock.

Our mind is very generous: it will give us what we spend the most time fixating on, whether positive or negative. However, we so often come back to the negative.

Brain neuroplasticity is the ability of the brain to create new neural pathways that we can train to become stronger and more positive as we reprogramme more positive thoughts and a mindset that is more beneficial for us. We can get the brain thinking in new ways, along new neural pathways that support our goals of abundance, healing and self-care.

Just as we programmed ourselves into a negative mindset, we have the means to replace the doubts with positive seeds that grow positive thoughts. We have only to identify and be aware of the contents of our thoughts and we can start by retelling the story and changing those old neural pathways to form new positive pathways that align more with our heart's desires.

By focusing on what you need to release, emptying out the old stuff that no longer serves us, by putting down our thoughts and feelings on paper, we tap into a source of tremendous power to shift to the positive and set up for success (whatever that means to us). When we give to ourselves first by journaling our innermost feelings and thoughts, before the demands of family, work and life kick in, we can start the day fresh, whole and focused on what is important that day.

Some days the thing to release may be the need to release anything at all. It may be time to let goodness in rather than let anything out. Let your intuition guide you. By identifying the good (that may not always be for our higher good, just saying), the bad, sad, mad parts, the ugly bits we hold tight like a fist that stop the light pouring in, we begin to develop true attention and discernment. We can then bring our intention in to purify the process.

A healthy self-evaluation process can uncover illusions and self-deceptions that don't serve us, allowing us to be real with ourselves and rip that Band-Aid off so our wounds can heal. There are no mistakes in any of this, just lessons learned and freedom found.

Once we give an honest account of what may need to go (remembering that all that is meant for us will never pass us by) we can release what holds us back and rest in what remains. We have space to connect with the blessings of this release and be grateful.

First let's look at all the ways we can keep ourselves stuck and perpetuate that 'stinking thinking'?

Mindset: a feeling that I'm not good enough, I don't deserve that, they must have made a mistake; that inner critic that says I'm going to fail or @#uck up. The ways we judge ourselves as bad, unattractive and shame ourselves. The guilt, fears, resentment we heap at ourselves and others; the pain of heartbreak, betrayal that we didn't deserve but was meted out by someone who was in pain themselves and needed to put it somewhere outside themselves to get rid of it and perhaps you were an easy target.

So many ways we beat ourselves up when we are the only true best friend we have ever had and will ever have- loyal for a lifetime. So, isn't it time to let that old story go and release that stuff we make into a far bigger story than it needs to be?

It's time to lighten our load and move through healing and out the other side to transformation!

This exercise can be spoken into your Smartphone so you can relax and use it as a guided meditation to identify blockages in the energy centres of the body, breathe through any knots and release. When we relax, our mind will naturally go to the places like the heart or the belly of the throat where we may be experiencing blockages. Below I give you an overview of the qualities associated with the chakras so you can get a sense if you are out of balance in those areas and a few suggestions to balance out the area or the feeling.

First let's try out the exercise.

Get comfortable, sit in a chair with feet flat on the floor, or cross-legged sitting on a cushion or if you must lie down try not to fall asleep. Close your eyes. Hunch your shoulders towards your ears then breathe out and release the shoulder blades so they melt down your back and tuck into their natural pockets, away from the ears.

Take 3 deep breaths in through the nose and sigh it out through the mouth then three more breaths counting in for 3, holding for 3 then breathing out for 3.

Now settle in to your natural, spontaneous, gentle breath. Relax your head and neck and move down through the different parts of your body all the way to your toes, breathing in relaxation and breathing out any tension. Identify as you scan down, where in your body you may be holding tension. Visualise it as a knot unravelling, as a veil lifting and blowing away in the wind or any way that allows it to soften and dissolve. Look in those corners and crevices of the body, under the ribs, in the pelvis, between the shoulder blades, around the jaw and back of the neck.

Once you've moved down from the top of the head, noticing any sensations and places where the energy isn't flowing freely, where the skin tingles, tickles, is hot or cool- all the way down to your toes, then take your awareness up to your mid chest, to the heart space and feel what is going on there. There may be hurts and sadness that arise or just a warm sense of calm and relaxation. Notice where you feel any feelings in your body. Our thoughts can also get stuck in our cells and tissues when we tense against them at times of grief and shock. Simply observe what is true for you. Breathe through it; let go of judgement about outcomes, it's just an exercise to notice what may feel stuck or blocked or trapped that you need to release in this present moment.

Take your time and when you are ready gently breathe out and send the breath to the extremities of your fingers and toes and notice how much more relaxed you are. Open your eyes and write down in your Journal what emotion, judgement, blockage or negative mindset you wish to release today.

Feeling lighter you can now ease into your day....

THE CHAKRAS
ENERGY HEALING

Looking at Chakras, colours & crystals to balance the Soul & Emotions

In the yogic chakra or energy system there are generally accepted to be 7 major chakras (meaning 'wheels' of energy) but you may only be drawn towards one or two areas that may be blocked or out of balance. Since our bodies grow out of our energy field it's important to release any energy that gets stuck. Out of balance chakras can create imbalance in the physical body and lead to illness. To correct imbalances just work out where you feel any blockages. These can be clues as to what is out of alignment and needs to be released or soothed.

The healing is so simple. In your meditation or trusting your intuition to go to the colour you are drawn to, simply breathe in this colour to the parts that need it or choose crystals of this colour to keep near you. If you locate the mental or emotional issue first, such as grief, then go to the guide and see that grief resides in the area of the chest around the heart and lungs, so breathe in the colour green to soothe and balance this area. Do what feels right for you. These are only suggestions to explore for yourself on your healing journey.

Below is a little further detail about each chakra and the associated elements, senses and qualities they embody. If a chakra is overactive it will need soothing and calming but if underactive then the below will help to activate and balance the chakra. Listen to your body/mind to tell you what postures are helping and what are hindering you on the day as these will change as your energy changes.

1. Mooladhara is the base or root chakra. Colour red. Sense of smell. Earth element. 4-petalled red lotus. Located below the tailbone or coccyx in the area of the perineum or cervix in women. As the base or foundation, it is connected to security, safety, stability and structure, our sense of belonging and our place here on this earth. If out of balance we may feel insecure or fearful and comforting yoga poses like pose of a child, or self care practices like wrapping ourselves in a warm blanket, or getting a hug may help.

A yoga pose to perform in balancing this chakra is squatting with hands in prayer pose or Half Moon standing pose balanced on one foot but this is an easier modified version where you can rest on one knee. Have one hand on the floor below your shoulder and lift the other up in a direct line above as you lift your leg and let it float up to hip height. Tilt your chin towards your chest to protect your neck then roll your head to gaze up at the upstretched hand. Breathe deeply into this pose for at least 5 breaths then change legs and do the other side.

2. Sacral chakra or Swadhistana (behind the pubic bone) Colour orange. Sense of taste. Water element. 6 petalled orange/vermillion lotus. It is the source of pleasure, creativity, connected to reproduction, passion, elimination and sexuality. When out of balance we can feel out of our flow in life, experience trust issues, behave cold and distant towards others or experience the opposite and be overly needy and dependent. Imbalance of the second chakra can manifest on a physical level through urinary issues, kidney problems, gynaecological problems and lower back pain.

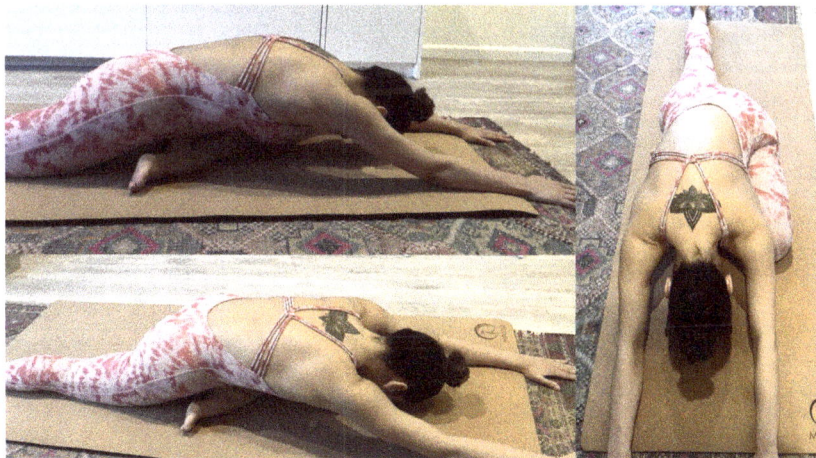

Yoga poses to try can include hip opening exercises like pigeon to let go of physical tension and release emotional blockages, thus stimulating and balancing your sacral chakra. Balancing poses such as Kakasana (Crow Pose) and standing poses like Trikonasana (Triangle Pose) are also effective poses.

For sleeping pigeon pose: start in Downward Facing Dog. With an exhale bend your left knee towards your chest and place your left knee on the floor in between your hands, left ankle behind right wrist (or adjust if your knees are dodgy and don't strain). Lower your right knee to the floor, sliding your leg back so that both hips are near the floor. Untuck the back toes. Check that your back leg is extended straight behind you. Rise onto your fingertips and lengthen your spine. Stay here for a few breaths. Slowly walk your hands forward with an exhale and rest your forehead on the floor or wherever it can (use a bolster or cushion to rest your head on if needed).

Hold the pose and take slow, deep breaths. Tuck your back toes under and carefully push yourself back to Downward Facing Dog with an exhale. Change sides.

3. Manipura ('jewel in the city' in Sanskrit) or the solar plexus chakra is slightly above the navel towards the spine; it is the seat of our digestive fire and associated with the element of fire, the colour orange, the ten-petalled yellow lotus and our sense of sight. It is associated with power, drive, confidence, taking action in the world. When in balance, it influences how well we express our confidence, sense of self-worth, purpose and motivation in the world. If stuck you may feel a lack of power, even powerlessness and lying down with hands on belly and breathing gently in and out of your navel may help.

Cobra pose will stretch and open manipura or a twist such as reverse warrior pose or boat pose.

4. Anahata chakra or the heart centre is in the mid chest above the sternum, to the right of the actual heart and in Sanskrit it means 'unstruck sound'. Element is air, the sense of touch and the 12 petalled green or blue lotus. Qualities: love, compassion, forgiveness, empathy, kindness. Out of

balance can express as lack of generosity, cold-heartedness, unforgiving. Poses: Bridge pose, warrior 2, 1-legged prayer pose with hands together at the heart space.

5. Vishuddhi or the throat chakra in the area behind the throat is the seat of self-expression and how we speak, communicate and express ourselves in the world. Its colour is deep blue and corresponding element is Akasha (space) or ether. Sense of hearing and the 16 petalled blue/purple lotus. It is linked to the thyroid gland and is a psychic centre of purification. When balanced there is a clear voice, a talent for singing and speech, balanced and calm thoughts. When this is blocked, we may have trouble speaking our truth to others or experience feelings of anxiety, lack of freedom, restriction, thyroid and throat problems. There may be physically unfounded manifestations of swallowing problems and speech impediments.

Yoga practise to try: Sphinx pose. Laying down on your stomach with your feet together, slide your forearms parallel on the floor and lift your chest off the floor so you are resting on your forearms forward with elbows on the ground in line with your shoulders, head upright and feel your throat open. Breathe gently with ujjayi breath (the sound a baby makes when it is sleeping- it sounds like a soft whispering breath at the throat that you can hear faintly and balances the nervous system).

Another pose to try is cat pose, rest on hands and knees. Lift your head, opening the throat & shine the chest forward as you dip the spine then tilt the chin towards your chest as you arch the spine and continue dipping and arching the spine like a cat.

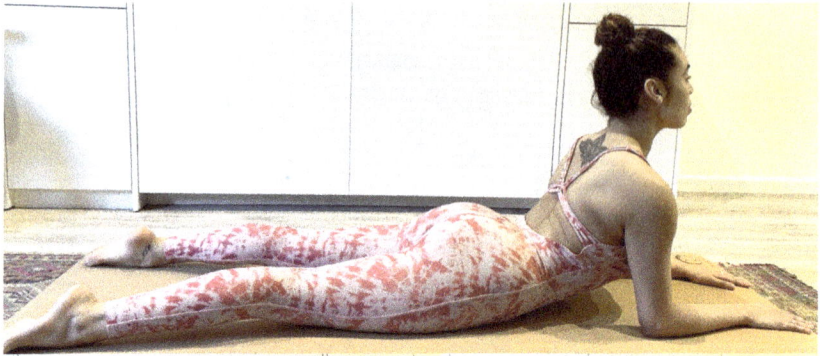

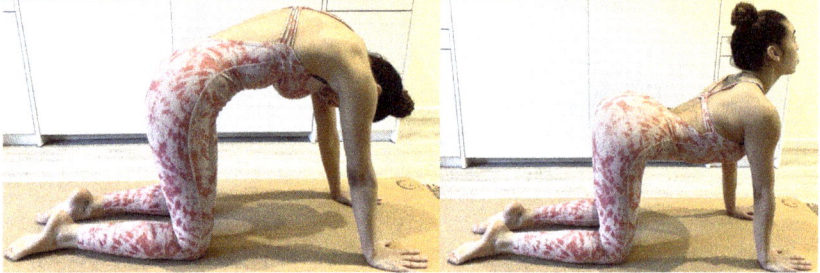

6. Ajna chakra is the third eye and located near the pineal gland in the centre of the head, above the top of the spine and midway between the ears. It is associated with the colour indigo and the sense of sight and the 2 petalled violet/silver lotus. It is the command and integration centre between how we operate and function in the physical world and our higher intuition and spiritual dimension of being. It controls and energizes the pituitary gland, the endocrine glands and the brain and is responsible for the health of your skin to a certain extent. When balanced there is self-reflection, intuition, wisdom, creativity, inspiration and insights but when imbalanced there can be a lack of clarity, mental stagnation, migraines, imbalance, overthinking or not having a clear vision for one's life.

Yoga practise to try:
Bhramari or humming bee breath. Sit comfortably with spine, head and neck aligned then tilt your chin down slightly and bring your elbows up level with your ears. Plug your index fingers of each hand lightly against the small outer flaps of your ears. Breathe out with a hum and hear the humming exhalation resonate in the centre of the head. Breathe in then hum out the exhale again. Continue for 7 rounds and then take your fingers out and feel the soothing effects of this sound bath on the brain and ajna chakra in the centre of the head.

7. Sahasrara is the crown chakra and the entry point for divine inspiration and downloads from spirit. It is represented by pure white light or a violet colour and the 1000 petalled white lotus. The seed mantra of Sahasrara Chakra is AUM. This chakra is considered to influence brain functions such as memory, intelligence, and focus. When balanced it brings spiritual understanding and peace with a clear perspective. Unbalanced or blocked, you may experience disillusionment, boredom, melancholy, and restlessness.

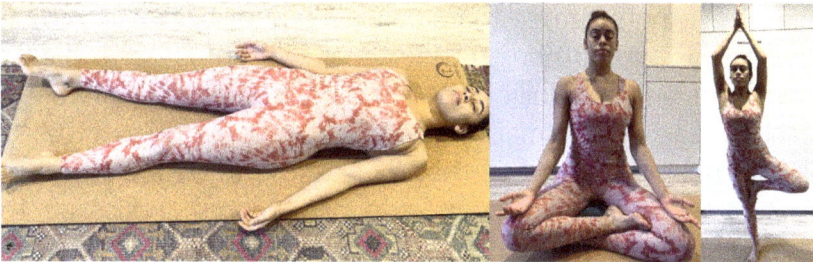

Yoga practises for this chakra include yoga nidra for relaxation and silence, lying down in corpse pose (shavasana) pictured, meditation with a gentle focus on receiving light in through that chakra and down through the central axis of the spine into the earth to ground you or poses such as tree pose.

Further thoughts on Healing

Healing happens from the inside out. Unhealthy thoughts create unhealthy patterns of behaviour and attract more of the same. When our mind and thoughts tend to the negative, we project this into the external world and start creating circumstances that back up our reasons for feeling fearful or expecting the worst. This is a clue that the mind needs to be washed and cleaned, just as we do for the body. Meditation helps purify the mind.

In any situation ask if this expands and lightens me or contracts me and weighs me down? I'm not referring to those tasks that are unpleasant but need to be done for us to have a good life- the tax returns, the bills paid- these are necessary. I mean the people, places, things that erode joy, self esteem, that cause us to feel less than- often they are our own beliefs about ourselves: I don't deserve that, I am not enough, when the truth is you always were and always will be!

A common healing is the healing needed around forgiveness, of self and others. We are all story tellers and the stories we tell ourselves in the privacy of our heads can often develop into negative thought patterns that reinforce fears, insecurities, resentments and guilt. Having the courage and honesty to reflect on how our unhealthy stories keep us small, stuck and blaming others rather than taking responsibility for having created or contributed to the scenario open us up to bigger questions and possibilities. WHAT IF I am not my story and I can imagine it as a small helpless bug or speck of dust sitting in the palm of my hand that I can blow away? WHAT IF I reimagine a positive outcome and take the steps necessary to achieve it? WHAT IF my doubt and insecurity is just an illusion and I am far stronger and more powerful than I realise? WHAT IF TODAY I think and act towards myself with love and kindness first and foremost, and see what happens?

Meditation

Meditation is one of the best ways I know to purify, ease and heal the mind. When we sit still and observe the thoughts, we start to observe what the yogis call the 'monkey mind'. It goes off in one direction, then another. The nature of the mind is to be restless. We can liken it to the glass of dirty water that is cloudy to begin, when we shake it up, but in time the sediment, the heavy thoughts, settle to the bottom and we start to see its clarity and true nature.

When we sit and watch without reacting to whatever comes up in the mind, a little like a patient mother keeping a loving eye out on her young, active toddler who can't keep still. When we are patient with ourselves, eventually the thoughts slow down, and we develop a calm detachment from them. We see them like clouds skimming across the surface of the sky of our mind. They come and go but don't change the vast, spacious nature of the open mind. We can watch the turbulence subside and as resistance falls away, we begin to access our intuition and higher mind and rest in the peace of silence and connecting with our true selves. Healing and peace unfold from the subtle to the gross dimensions of being, from the mind to the emotions to the body and out to calm our external environment as we express this deep peace.

Apart from meditation, other healing aids to soothe a restless mind and reduce stress include grounding and centring yourself by walking barefoot on grass or at the beach, swimming, taking a shower and imagining washing off any troubles, getting a massage, doing an act of random kindness or service for someone without needing reward, having a good cry, nourishing your body with a healthy meal. If you are down and troubled or feel weighed down with grief or resentment, then the H'opono'pono Hawaiian prayer below is an incredible tool for healing the heart.

Gratitude

After we release and let go and decide what needs to be healed, it's important to counter any sense of loss by uplifting and nourishing our spirit. We do this by remembering all the things we have in our life that we are grateful for. The Divine appreciates us and showers us with more abundance and blessings when we count our blessings and show thanks and humility for all the things we have in our life.

Gratitude grounds and humbles us in the present moment. It covers the spectrum from what we have learned that may have been unpleasant and painful but which leads us to a new beginning and a fresh start long overdue to things that we feel lucky to enjoy – the air we breathe to the birds singing outside our window. Gratitude paves the way to connecting with the richness of what we have right now, the blessings in our life. It leads to us feeling whole, appreciative and abundant. It moves us away from comparing ourselves to others and grounds us in bounty rather than lack. It demands us to stay in the present rather than look over our shoulder at the past or forward into a future that we cannot control. Now, this very moment, when we feel ourselves breathing and our heart beating, is the only time we have to impact life for the better. The only real opportunity we can build on in a truly positive way.

Gratitude & Connection Exercise

When we are having doubts and insecurities, feeling a lack in our lives, clinging to the past or contracting around perceived problems that are future-based and which we cannot control; it's time to stop and let the love, abundance and support back in with this simple exercise. You could say it into the voice memo recorder on your phone and play it back as a guided visualisation.

1. Get comfortable, ideally sitting in a chair or cross legged on a cushion- wherever you are comfortable. Try not to lie down or you may go to sleep, but if that's what you need: do it! However you feel most relaxed.

2. Take 3 deep breaths in through your nose and out through your mouth to release any worries and settle yourself. Feel grounded and soften your breath so it comes easily and smoothly.

3. Imagine yourself in a safe, beautiful, peaceful place inside or outside. Hear the soothing sounds around you, smell the

heavenly fragrance in the air and ease into the relaxation of your special sanctuary. Ensure this sanctuary is spacious yet safe.

4. See yourself sitting in the centre of a circle that has 3 outer rings around it and each ring can expand to support those who enter it.

5. In the first circle around you, imagine all the living friends and family and any pets that have loved and supported you this week, this month, this year and in the past. See them come forward to sit around you silently as they enter the inner circle. They are here to surround and support you with their love, attention and good wishes.

6. In the second circle around them, bring in others who have said a kind word or helped you in any way. It can be teachers, shopkeepers, doctors, people from your neighbourhood- bring them all in.

7. Then into that second circle, welcome in all the people who have supported you, grown the food you eat, built the roads you drive on, created the house and furniture you enjoy, supplied you with a good or service that benefited you in some way.

8. Around this circle, in the third outer circle, place all your ancestors who contributed to your existence- the grandmothers and fathers going way back down the family line, known and unknown. You would not be here but for them. Send your gratitude to them.

9. Now truly see this incredible group of people, as far as they eye can see, sitting around you, connect to receiving and filling yourself up with their love and support. You are not alone, and you have been assisted in some way by every person in this circle. You have received and had all your needs met by them from the food they helped put on your table to the water you shower with to the ancestors who created you and there is SO much to be thankful for!

Now, take a deep breath in and fill your heart to the brim with this beautiful feeling of support and gratitude and then prepare to gently open your eyes and take this abundance with you into your day.......

Inspiration

Inspiration is the in breath and expiration is the out breath. We have expelled and released what no longer serves us. Now it's time to breathe in what does! Inspiration is also feeling uplifted in our thoughts, our emotions, our actions, dreams and goals; an enthusiasm we get from something or someone which gives us new and creative ideas. When we hear, see, feel or experience something that sets us on fire, energises us, fuels our passion, then we have been blessed with inspiration.

Each day has a footnote quote designed to inspire you or shift your perspective and help you start the day feeling energised.

If you need more inspiration then put on a playlist of your favourite songs, listen to an inspiring podcast, google inspiring quotes or meditate on what your personal sources of inspiration are and aim to nourish yourself with a source of your favourite inspiration each day.

What I aim to give that I want to Attract Today

I only recently heard about the Law of Resonance by Michael Beckwith which builds on the Law of Attraction that affirms 'like attracts like'. If we think positive thoughts we attract positive outcomes. If we think and dwell on negative thoughts and actions, we get more of the same.

Beckwith takes it a step further when he talks about the way we attract those situations, people and things in our life that vibrate or resonate with who and what we are not simply what we want or desire. Thus, it's not simply that we can attract the things we want into our lives by simply wanting them. We have to become that which we seek through love, forgiveness, gratitude, generosity, acceptance and all the ways we can lift our vibration which will naturally and effortlessly call or draw to us those things which are resonating at that same uplifted frequency. Conversely at those times when we are feeling very negative, we often notice we seem to attract an apparent string of bad luck or negative situations. It works both ways, depending on our energy field and how we are resonating.

It follows that when we strive to visualise and manifest a positive, abundant life by focusing on higher vibration frequencies generated by qualities like love and kindness and giving to others, we act as a magnet to attract those same qualities into our life.

So, decide and visualise what qualities you commit to sharing today that will lift your vibratory frequency, helping you to resonate at this higher level and watch what magic and miracles that attracts. Journal your results and watch life TRANSFORM.

My Wisdom & Insight Toolkit

There are three inspiring poems and prayers I read regularly that woke me up spiritually and motivated me to change for the better. The first is by Marianne Williamson and was adapted by Nelson Mandela in his 1994 Inaugural Speech:

"Our deepest fear is not that we are inadequate. Our deepest fear is that we are powerful beyond measure. It is our light, not our darkness that most frightens us. We ask ourselves, 'Who am I to be brilliant, gorgeous, talented, fabulous?' Who are you not to be? You are a child of God. Your playing small does not serve the world. There is nothing enlightened about shrinking so that other people won't feel insecure around you. We are all meant to shine, as children do. We were born to make manifest the glory of God that is within us. It's not just in some of us; it's in everyone. And as we let our own light shine, we unconsciously give other people permission to do the same. As we are liberated from our own fear, our presence automatically liberates others."

Wow- it's OK for me to shine and that helps others to do the same- so simple, so profound. Indeed, who am I NOT to be the fabulous woman I was born to be and why waste another minute not living in my own light?! And shining it out so others can see their own unique ways forward....

The Serenity Prayer

The second poem is a short prayer that blew me away because it gave me a compass to check in whenever I had a problem that needed attention and guide me to whether I could impact it and influence the outcome for the better or whether it was beyond my control and best accepted and let go of. I tend to replace the word God with Divine but you can put Brahma, Allah, Christ, Aunt Betty- whoever you prefer in there and it works just as well.

I freaking LOVE these three simple lines from the AA 12 Step programme: The Serenity Prayer

God grant me the serenity to accept the things I cannot change,
The courage to change the things I can,
and the wisdom to know the difference.

Simple and so profound- it prods me to take responsibility for any messes I make, to stand up and speak out about the things that matter to me and let go of the rest....

Ho'opono'pono prayer

Finally, the simple but universal Hawaiian Ho'opono'pono prayer that brings me to tears whenever I say it and which I truly believe from my experience, has the capacity to heal any deep emotional pain in the heart, mind and spirit. It develops self-love, humility and forgiveness. It is a lullaby to the soul that speaks to our heart's desire to be loved, accepted, forgiven and at peace.

I'm sorry.
Please forgive me.
Thank you.
I love you.

Spend the next few minutes with your eyes closed, relaxed, comfortable and at ease. Take three deep breaths in through the nose and out through the mouth then soften your breath, bring your attention to the centre of your chest, your heart space. Begin to repeat it mentally to yourself for as long as you need until something changes. Watch what comes up then write your insights below:

I'm sorry, Please forgive me, Thank you, I love you

(Keep repeating until you feel it working; and it will. If it doesn't you may be in your head rather than connected to your heart so come back to it and try again later.)

....

....

....

....

....

Yoga is more than just pretzel postures!

"The yogis, abandoning attachment, act with body, mind, intelligence, and even with the senses, only for the purpose of purification."

Bhagavad Gita (Chapter 5, vs. 11)

Yoga is the art of bringing the different polarities existing in the body/mind into unity and restoring ease, balance, harmony, peace and health to every level of our being- mind, body and spirit.

In the words of a wise friend, Helen Scard:

"What's happening to our planet is actually reflected in us and vice-versa. We can look at global situations and feel that there isn't much we as individuals can do, or not know where to start. But we can start with ourselves, taking care of our health & happiness so that we can face the challenges that life on Earth brings. Would we like some help to get started?

Yes! it's fun to do things together - let's look at us and our relationship with the planet.........

We are the water. We see the Oceans and the beautiful creatures that live in the water ~ Our bodies are 70-80% water ~

We are the Fire. We see the Fire, feel the warmth and bask in the glow of the flames – We follow the Sun ~ our digestive fire breaks down our food to fuel our bodies ~

We are the Air. We see the Wind – we breathe the air – we can't live without it –

We are the Wood. We stand upon the Earth – we eat from her soil, we bathe in her waters, we build shelter from her trees ~ Our roots are deep and the Seasons bring change – a time for letting go, a time for new growth, a time to blossom, a time for rest, a time for sleep.

Our cells inside our bodies renew every 7 days so at any one time you are no more than 120 days old! Everything is always changing..... the cells in our bodies, the weather, our lives ~ and yet we witness nature bringing everything into balance.

Yoga is a practice of the imitation of nature – The Tree Pose, The Mountain Pose, The Bridge, Cat, Dog, Tiger, Fish, Hare, Salute to the Sun, Salute to the Moon, The wave of our breath, The Root of our spine...........

Yoga brings awareness, the postures Flow like water, from one to the next. We learn to go with the flow and we arrive without struggling or striving - just by Being and just by Breathing."

My go to yoga practises for transformation

These include meditation, yoga nidra with a sankalpa (positive resolve stated in the present tense e.g. I am calm, clear and relaxed)

Pranayama: Ujjayi breath, Kapalabhati, Nadi Shodhana, Bhramari (humming bee breath)

Asanas (poses) such as pose of a child, shoulder stand to halasana, warrior pose, trikonasana, kandarasana, ardha matsyendrasana, kati chakrasana, chakki chalana, Butterfly, pigeon, 1-legged prayer pose, shavasana (corpse pose).

Please modify any poses if you have back, knee or other health issues or seek the guidance of a yoga teacher.

Chanting Mantras for Healing and Transformation

- Mantras are sacred Sanskrit sounds (mantrikas meaning 'little mothers' as they are full of creative power) that are repeated aloud or mentally (as japa) for distinct purposes

- they call up divine aspects of our being, lift and lighten our vibration, heal the subtle energy body & purify negative thought patterns

- mantras like 'Om Namah Shivaya' saturate the aspirant in divine energy to facilitate enlightenment

- Can be sung as in kirtan, spoken or mentally repeated

- e.g. AUM is known as the universal sound of creation and a bija (seed) mantra relating to ajna chakra: used to transcend obstacles; Patanjali in his Yoga Sutras recommends mental AUM or OM chanting as a sadhana to overcome the obstacles to Samadhi (1:27-29)

- for mental clarity & wisdom: gayatri mantra; other gayatris are surya gayatri (good for skin diseases/allergies), rudra gayatri,vishnu gayatri which invoke the gods (refer to Mahanarayana Upanishad)

If I need healing or wish to send it to someone that is suffering (and have their permission) I light a candle and chant the Mahamrityunjaya mantra. This can be chanted at the bedside of someone who is ill or in hospital to assist healing.

Mahamrityunjaya Mantra is a verse of the Rigveda (RV 7.59.12):

Mahamritunjaya mantra

Om tryambkam yajamahe

Sugandhim pustivardhanam Urvarukamiva bandhanat Mrityormukshiyamamritat

Aum Shanti Shanti Shanti [Shanti means peace in Sanskrit]

Chant for health and wellbeing of self and others

We pay homage to the universal consciousness which nourishes all beings. May we be liberated from the death of ignorance through knowledge of our immortal essence, just as the cucumber is severed from the bondage of the vine.

Created with thanks to Mangrove Mountain Ashram and Satyananda Yoga

There are many versions on YouTube, but I like Sounds of Isha Maha Mrityunjaya Mantra [108 times] which takes 38 minutes.

The next mantra is for the mind, tranquillity and wisdom:

Gayatri mantra

Om bhur bhuva swaha
Tat savitur varenyam
Bhargo devasya dhimahi
Dhiyo yo nah prachodayat
Aum Shantih Shantih Shantih

The next mantra is to remove obstacles for times of distress and hardship:

Listen to the pronunciation as call and response on YouTube at Durgaadvaatrinshannaamamaalaa 32 Names of Durga (on channel Deteios Attikos, chanted by Swami Niranjan) 9:33 minutes

Durgha path

Durgha according to legend, emerged from the waters of the holy Ganga river as a spirit to defeat the buffalo demon Mahisasura and was given a physical form by all the gods put together. She is both derivative from the male divinities Brahma, Vishnu and Shiva and the true source of their inner power. She is also greater than any of them as she is created from all of them. Durga is usually depicted riding a lion and with 8 or 10 arms, each holding the special weapon of one of the gods. She is a powerful ally to have on your side in times of heartache, distress or hardship.

Chanting the 32 names of Durgha gives me greater strength and clarity to face any problems in life. She is the kick-arse Goddess of the Hindhu pantheon with no equal and in different forms she represents different aspects of the Divine Feminine. Visualise her beautiful form astride her lion and chant her names to access her magnificent power and empowerment!

Durga Path

32 names of Durga

1. Om DUR-gaa
2. Dur-gaar-ti sha-MA-ni
3. Dur-gaa-pad-vi-ni-vaa-RI-nii
4. Dur-ga-ma-cche-DI-nii
5. Dur-ga-saa-DHI-nii
6. Dur-ga-naa-SHI-nii
7. Dur-ga-TOD dhaa-RI-nii
8. Dur-ga-ni-HAN-trii
9. Dur-ga-maa-PA-haa
10. DUR-ga-ma-gyaa-NA-daa
11. Dur-ga-dai-tya-LO-ka-da-vaa-NA-laa
12. Dur-ga-MAA
13. Dur-ga-MAA-LO-kaa
14. Dur-ga-maat-MA-SV A-roo-PI-nii
15. Dur-ga-maar-ga-PRA-daa
16. Dur-ga-ma-VID-yaa
17. Dur-ga-maa-SHRI-taa
18. Dur-ga-MA-GYAA-NA-sam-sthaa-naa
19. Dur-ga-ma-dhyaa-NA-BHAA-si-nii
20. Dur-ga-mo-haa
21. Dur-ga-MA-gaa
22. Dur-ga-maa-THA-SWA-roo-PI-nii
23. Dur-ga-maa-SU-RA-sam-HAN-trii
24. Dur-ga-maa-YU-DHA-dha-RI-nii

25. DUR-ga-MAAN-gii
26. Dur-ga-MA-taa
27. Dur-ga-myaa
28. Dur-ga-mesh-VA-rii
29. DUR-ga-BHII-MA
30. Dur-ga-bhaa-maa
31. Dur-ga-bhaa
32. Dur-ga-daa-ri-n

Translation

1. Reliever of difficulties
2. Who puts difficulties at peace
3. Dispeller of difficult adversities
4. Who cuts down difficulties
5. The performer of discipline to dispel difficulties
6. The destroyer of difficulties
7. Who holds the whip to difficulties
8. Who sends difficulties to ruin
9. Who measures difficulties
10. Who makes difficulties unconscious
11. Who destroys the world of difficult thoughts
12. Mother of difficulties
13. The perception of difficulties
14. The intrinsic nature of the soul of difficulties
15. Who searches through difficulties
16. The knowledge of difficulties
17. The extrication of difficulties
18. The continued of existence of difficulties
19. Whose meditation remains brilliant when in difficulties
20. Who deludes difficulties
21. Who resolves difficulties
22. Who is the instrinsic nature of the object of difficulties
23. The annihilator of the egotism of difficulties
24. Bearer of the weapon against difficulties
25. The refinery of difficulties
26. Who is beyond difficulties
27. Accessible with difficulty

28.The empress of difficulties
29.Who is terrible to difficulties
30.The lady of difficulties
31.The illuminator of difficulties
32.Who cuts off difficulties

I hope some of these tools and insights will help you on your journey and your journaling to transformation.

Melissa xox

Date: /   /   I'm Feeling:

I release:

....

....

....

Today's healing:

....

....

I'm grateful for:

....

....

....

I'm inspired by:

....

....

What I give out that I wish to attract today:

....

....

....

Dreams/Notes:

....

....

....

....

I woke up beautiful, smart, sexy and funny AGAIN! This is getting out of hand!
message on a milkshake container

Date: /   /   I'm Feeling:

I release:
....
....
....
....

Today's healing:
....
....
....

I'm grateful for:
....
....
....
....

I'm inspired by:
....
....
....

What I give out that I wish to attract today:
....
....
....
....

Dreams/Notes:
....
....
....
....
....

A woman is like a tea bag — you never know how strong she is until she gets in hot water. Eleanor Roosevelt

Date: / / | I'm Feeling:

I release:

....
....
....

Today's healing:

....
....

I'm grateful for:

....
....
....

I'm inspired by:

....
....

What I give out that I wish to attract today:

....
....
....

Dreams/Notes:

....
....
....
....
....

May all beings be safe, healthy, happy, free and peaceful in their heart of hearts.
Adapted from the Buddhist prayer

Date: /   /

I'm Feeling:

I release:

....
....
....

Today's healing:

....
....

I'm grateful for:

....
....
....

I'm inspired by:

....
....

What I give out that I wish to attract today:

....
....
....

Dreams/Notes:

....
....
....
....

I do not expect anything from others so their actions cannot be in opposition to my wishes. Swami Sri Yukteswar Autobiography of a Yogi

Date: /   /   I'm Feeling:

I release:

....

....

....

Today's healing:

....

....

I'm grateful for:

....

....

....

I'm inspired by:

....

....

What I give out that I wish to attract today:

....

....

....

Dreams/Notes:

....

....

....

....

Taking joy in living is a woman's best cosmetic. Rosalind Russell

Date: /   / | I'm Feeling:

I release:

....
....
....

Today's healing:

....
....

I'm grateful for:

....
....
....

I'm inspired by:

....
....

What I give out that I wish to attract today:

....
....
....

Dreams/Notes:

....
....
....

Like the pearl in the oyster, great beauty is created through the friction and challenges of our life. Sometimes we don't see it until our courage to speak our truth and choose love over fear, shucks open that oyster to reveal the luminous beauty, strength, self worth and resilience of the hidden pearl. The Author

Date: / / I'm Feeling:

I release:

....
....
....

Today's healing:

....
....

I'm grateful for:

....
....
....

I'm inspired by:

....
....

What I give out that I wish to attract today:

....
....
....

Dreams/Notes:

....
....
....
....

When we see the drama of our life clearly, we can liberate ourselves from it. Move from being the actor in a Shakespearean drama to being the audience watching the play unfold. Detach & enjoy the comedy, tragedy, romance and mystery of our lives without being a slave to the action. This is freedom. The Author

Date: / /	I'm Feeling:

I release:

....
....
....
....

Today's healing:

....
....
....

I'm grateful for:

....
....
....
....

I'm inspired by:

....
....
....

What I give out that I wish to attract today:

....
....
....
....

Dreams/Notes:

....
....
....
....

Damn I look good in that mirror. My eyes sparkle, this face is my best friend and we're ready to take on life! Confidence is an aphrodisiac. The Author (who wears glasses lol!)

Date: /   /   I'm Feeling:

I release:

....

....

....

Today's healing:

....

....

I'm grateful for:

....

....

....

I'm inspired by:

....

....

What I give out that I wish to attract today:

....

....

....

Dreams/Notes:

....

....

....

....

Take the whole away from the whole and only the whole remains. Om peace
From the Isha Upanishad. A reminder we are whole and complete just as we are.

Date: /   /   I'm Feeling:

I release:
....
....
....

Today's healing:
....
....

I'm grateful for:
....
....
....

I'm inspired by:
....
....

What I give out that I wish to attract today:
....
....
....

Dreams/Notes:
....
....
....
....

Divine (Source/God) I am turning this day over to you. Your will, not mine, be done.
Please guide me to think, say and do the right thing today for the highest good of
all concerned. The Author & Rebecca Manning

Date: / /   I'm Feeling:

I release:

....

....

....

Today's healing:

....

....

I'm grateful for:

....

....

....

I'm inspired by:

....

....

What I give out that I wish to attract today:

....

....

....

Dreams/Notes:

....

....

....

....

I went to the supermarket to buy a new attitude but realized this one's just fine thanks! The Author

Date: /   /   I'm Feeling:

I release:

....

....

....

....

Today's healing:

....

....

I'm grateful for:

....

....

....

I'm inspired by:

....

....

What I give out that I wish to attract today:

....

....

....

Dreams/Notes:

....

....

....

....

....

Don't fear death, fear not living your best life with no regrets until your death.
Unknown

Date: / /   I'm Feeling:

I release:

....
....
....

Today's healing:

....
....

I'm grateful for:

....
....
....

I'm inspired by:

....
....

What I give out that I wish to attract today:

....
....
....

Dreams/Notes:

....
....
....
....

How do we discover new oceans unless we have the courage to lose sight of the shore? Unknown

Date: /   / | I'm Feeling:

I release:
....
....
....

Today's healing:
....
....

I'm grateful for:
....
....
....

I'm inspired by:
....
....

What I give out that I wish to attract today:
....
....
....

Dreams/Notes:
....
....
....
....

I am unique, whole and unrepeatable. No one can live my life, think these thoughts or make these decisions but me. I don't always get it right and I don't have to. I'm deliciously human and the flaws that make me who I am, have just as much right to be here as my magnificence does! I breathe out resistance and know I am enough. The Author

Date: / /	I'm Feeling:

I release:

....

....

....

Today's healing:

....

....

I'm grateful for:

....

....

....

I'm inspired by:

....

....

What I give out that I wish to attract today:

....

....

....

Dreams/Notes:

....

....

....

....

My playing small does not serve others. I give myself permission to expand my horizons and shine my light as I create my own unique path through the darkness. When strength and courage fail me, I remind myself I'm never alone. These are the times I am carried though hardship in the arms of the Divine. I am safe and all will be well. The Author

Date: / /   I'm Feeling:

I release:
....
....
....

Today's healing:
....
....

I'm grateful for:
....
....
....

I'm inspired by:
....
....

What I give out that I wish to attract today:
....
....
....

Dreams/Notes:
....
....
....
....

Within the cause and core of my problems lies the source of my solution to them. I am patient and look deeper. The Author

Date: / /   I'm Feeling:

I release:
....
....
....

Today's healing:
....
....

I'm grateful for:
....
....
....

I'm inspired by:
....
....

What I give out that I wish to attract today:
....
....
....

Dreams/Notes:
....
....
....
....
....

The Serenity Prayer: Give me the courage to change the things I can, the serenity to accept the things I can't, and the wisdom to know the difference. From the 12 Step program

Date: /   /   I'm Feeling:

I release:

....
....
....

Today's healing:

....
....

I'm grateful for:

....
....
....

I'm inspired by:

....
....

What I give out that I wish to attract today:

....
....
....

Dreams/Notes:

....
....
....
....

I have more fun watching my money bring joy to others than watching it stagnate.
Giving gives to me and what I give with joy and generosity in my heart returns to
me a hundredfold. The Author

Date: / /

I'm Feeling:

I release:

Today's healing:

I'm grateful for:

I'm inspired by:

What I give out that I wish to attract today:

Dreams/Notes:

If you close your mind in judgements and traffic with desires, your heart will be troubled. If you keep your mind from judging and aren't led by the senses, your heart will find peace. Tao te Ching

Date: /   /

I'm Feeling:

I release:

....
....
....

Today's healing:

....
....

I'm grateful for:

....
....
....

I'm inspired by:

....
....

What I give out that I wish to attract today:

....
....
....

Dreams/Notes:

....
....
....
....
....

Always keep your feet on the ground in case someone needs to lean on you.
Michael Powell

Date: /   /   I'm Feeling:

I release:

Today's healing:

I'm grateful for:

I'm inspired by:

What I give out that I wish to attract today:

Dreams/Notes:

What can we say when everything has been spoken....silence becomes the only way forward. Rebecca Manning

Date: /   /   I'm Feeling:

I release:

....

....

....

Today's healing:

....

....

I'm grateful for:

....

....

....

I'm inspired by:

....

....

What I give out that I wish to attract today:

....

....

....

Dreams/Notes:

....

....

....

....

Raise your standard of living by raising your standard of giving. Unknown

Date: /   /   I'm Feeling:

I release:

....
....
....

Today's healing:

....
....

I'm grateful for:

....
....
....

I'm inspired by:

....
....

What I give out that I wish to attract today:

....
....
....

Dreams/Notes:

....
....
....
....
....

No-knowing is true knowledge. Presuming is a disease. First realise that you are sick; then you can move towards health. Tao te Ching

Date: / /	I'm Feeling:

I release:

....

....

....

Today's healing:

....

....

I'm grateful for:

....

....

....

I'm inspired by:

....

....

What I give out that I wish to attract today:

....

....

....

Dreams/Notes:

....

....

....

....

If things aren't working in my life and I approach life the same way I did in the past, I'm headed for the same result. I give myself permission to let the fresh energy of a new approach flood in to cleanse and create a new perspective. What is outgrown I release and what is meant for me will come. The Author

Date: / /	I'm Feeling:

I release:

....

....

....

....

Today's healing:

....

....

....

I'm grateful for:

....

....

....

....

I'm inspired by:

....

....

....

What I give out that I wish to attract today:

....

....

....

....

Dreams/Notes:

....

....

....

....

Thoughts are things; they have tremendous power. Thoughts of doubt and fear are pathways to failure. When you conquer negative attitudes of doubt and fear you conquer failure. Thoughts crystallise into habit and habit solidifies into circumstances.
Brian Adams How to Succeed

Date: /   /   I'm Feeling:

I release:

....

....

....

Today's healing:

....

....

I'm grateful for:

....

....

....

I'm inspired by:

....

....

What I give out that I wish to attract today:

....

....

....

Dreams/Notes:

....

....

....

....

....

Don't go to bed without doing a kind, generous act towards another: you'll become a paragon of generosity even if it's just so you can get a little sleep! Unknown

Date: /   /   I'm Feeling:

I release:
....
....
....

Today's healing:
....
....

I'm grateful for:
....
....
....

I'm inspired by:
....
....

What I give out that I wish to attract today:
....
....
....

Dreams/Notes:
....
....
....
....

Those who know don't talk. Those who talk don't know. Tao te Ching

Date: /   /   I'm Feeling:

I release:
....
....
....
....

Today's healing:
....
....
....

I'm grateful for:
....
....
....
....

I'm inspired by:
....
....
....

What I give out that I wish to attract today:
....
....
....
....

Dreams/Notes:
....
....
....
....
....

I am outside my comfort zone right now and it feels so good, thank you.
Rebecca Manning

Date: / /   I'm Feeling:

I release:

....
....

Today's healing:

....
....

I'm grateful for:

....
....

I'm inspired by:

....
....

What I give out that I wish to attract today:

....
....

Dreams/Notes:

....
....
....
....

The impossible is possible when people align with you. When you do things with people, not against them, the amazing resources of the Higher Self within are mobilized. Gita Bellin

Date: /   /   I'm Feeling:

I release:

....
....
....

Today's healing:

....
....

I'm grateful for:

....
....
....

I'm inspired by:

....
....

What I give out that I wish to attract today:

....
....
....

Dreams/Notes:

....
....
....
....
....

There is no greater illusion than fear...whoever can see through fear will always be safe. Tao te Ching

Date: /   /   I'm Feeling:

I release:

....
....
....

Today's healing:

....
....

I'm grateful for:

....
....
....

I'm inspired by:

....
....

What I give out that I wish to attract today:

....
....
....

Dreams/Notes:

....
....
....
....
....

Never be afraid to tread the path alone. Know which is your path and follow it wherever it may lead you; do not feel you have to follow in someone else's footsteps. Eileen Caddy *Footprints on the Path*

Date: /   /   I'm Feeling:

I release:
....
....
....

Today's healing:
....
....

I'm grateful for:
....
....
....

I'm inspired by:
....
....

What I give out that I wish to attract today:
....
....
....

Dreams/Notes:
....
....
....
....

To find yourself. Think for yourself. Socrates

Date: /   /   I'm Feeling:

I release:
....
....
....

Today's healing:
....
....

I'm grateful for:
....
....
....

I'm inspired by:
....
....

What I give out that I wish to attract today:
....
....
....

Dreams/Notes:
....
....
....
....
....

Stride forward with a firm, steady step knowing with a deep, certain inner knowing that you will reach every goal you set yourselves, that you will achieve every action. Eileen Caddy *Footprints on the Path*

Date: /   /   I'm Feeling:

I release:

....

....

....

Today's healing:

....

....

I'm grateful for:

....

....

....

I'm inspired by:

....

....

What I give out that I wish to attract today:

....

....

....

Dreams/Notes:

....

....

....

....

....

Inner peace can be reached only when we practice forgiveness. Forgiveness is the letting go of the past, and is therefore the means for correcting our misperceptions.
Gerald G. Jampolsky *Love is Letting go of Fear*

Date: /   /   I'm Feeling:

I release:
....
....
....

Today's healing:
....
....

I'm grateful for:
....
....
....

I'm inspired by:
....
....

What I give out that I wish to attract today:
....
....
....

Dreams/Notes:
....
....
....
....

Sometimes life changes our game plan, throwing everything into chaos, but if we surrender control and allow the universe to place us where we need to be, the journey can be so much more rewarding. Rebecca Manning

Date: /   /

I'm Feeling:

I release:

....
....
....

Today's healing:

....
....

I'm grateful for:

....
....
....

I'm inspired by:

....
....

What I give out that I wish to attract today:

....
....
....

Dreams/Notes:

....
....
....
....

To unleash the hidden power of your mind involves your willingness to endure perspiration as well as inspiration. Vishen Lakhiani in *Silva Ultramind Method*

Date: /   / | I'm Feeling:

I release:
....
....
....

Today's healing:
....
....

I'm grateful for:
....
....
....

I'm inspired by:
....
....

What I give out that I wish to attract today:
....
....
....

Dreams/Notes:
....
....
....
....
....

Be the change you wish to see in the world. Mahatma Gandhi

Date: /   /   I'm Feeling:

I release:

....

....

....

Today's healing:

....

....

I'm grateful for:

....

....

....

I'm inspired by:

....

....

What I give out that I wish to attract today:

....

....

....

Dreams/Notes:

....

....

....

....

When you start seeing your worth, you'll find it harder to be around people who don't. Unknown

| Date: /   / | I'm Feeling: |

I release:

....

....

....

Today's healing:

....

....

I'm grateful for:

....

....

....

I'm inspired by:

....

....

What I give out that I wish to attract today:

....

....

....

Dreams/Notes:

....

....

....

....

....

Nothing is impossible. The word itself says 'I'm Possible!' Audrey Hepburn

Date: / /

I'm Feeling:

I release:

....

....

....

Today's healing:

....

....

I'm grateful for:

....

....

....

I'm inspired by:

....

....

What I give out that I wish to attract today:

....

....

....

Dreams/Notes:

....

....

....

A thousand candles can be lit from a single candle without the life of that candle being shortened. Go out and spread smiles, laughter and light that others will take to light the candles of joy in other's lives. This way you keep your original flame alight and spread it further than you can imagine. The Author

Date: /   /   I'm Feeling:

I release:

....

....

....

Today's healing:

....

....

I'm grateful for:

....

....

....

I'm inspired by:

....

....

What I give out that I wish to attract today:

....

....

....

Dreams/Notes:

....

....

....

....

There is only one courage and that is the courage to go on dying to the past, not to collect it, not to accumulate it, not to cling to it. We all cling to the past...and when we do, we become unavailable to the present. Bhagwan Shree Rajneesh
Walking in Zen, Sitting in Zen

Date: / /   I'm Feeling:

I release:

....
....
....

Today's healing:

....
....

I'm grateful for:

....
....
....
....

I'm inspired by:

....
....

What I give out that I wish to attract today:

....
....
....
....

Dreams/Notes:

....
....
....
....
....

Never be limited by other people's limited imaginations. Dr. Mae Jemison, *first female astronaut of colour in space*

Date: / /   I'm Feeling:

I release:

Today's healing:

I'm grateful for:

I'm inspired by:

What I give out that I wish to attract today:

Dreams/Notes:

Success is not final; Failure is not fatal. It is the courage to continue that counts.
Winston Churchill

Date: / /	I'm Feeling:

I release:

....

....

....

Today's healing:

....

....

I'm grateful for:

....

....

....

I'm inspired by:

....

....

What I give out that I wish to attract today:

....

....

....

Dreams/Notes:

....

....

....

....

There's a moment where you have to choose whether to be silent or stand up.
Malala Yousafzai, *Pakistani activist for female education*

Date: /   / | I'm Feeling:

I release:

....

....

....

Today's healing:

....

....

I'm grateful for:

....

....

....

I'm inspired by:

....

....

What I give out that I wish to attract today:

....

....

....

Dreams/Notes:

....

....

....

....

Every day may not always be a good day but we can always see the good in every day. Bhante Sujata

Date: /   /   I'm Feeling:

I release:
....
....
....

Today's healing:
....
....

I'm grateful for:
....
....
....

I'm inspired by:
....
....

What I give out that I wish to attract today:
....
....
....

Dreams/Notes:
....
....
....
....

You are braver than you believe, stronger than you seem, more beautiful than you imagine & more loved than you know. Unknown

Date: / / I'm Feeling:

I release:

Today's healing:

I'm grateful for:

I'm inspired by:

What I give out that I wish to attract today:

Dreams/Notes:

You can't separate peace from freedom because no one can be at peace unless he has his freedom. Malcolm X, *Human Rights Activist*

Date: /   /   I'm Feeling:

I release:

....
....
....

Today's healing:

....
....

I'm grateful for:

....
....
....

I'm inspired by:

....
....

What I give out that I wish to attract today:

....
....
....

Dreams/Notes:

....
....
....
....

Life shrinks or expands in proportion to one's courage. Anais Nin

Date: /   /

I'm Feeling:

I release:

....

....

Today's healing:

....

....

I'm grateful for:

....

....

I'm inspired by:

....

....

What I give out that I wish to attract today:

....

....

....

Dreams/Notes:

....

....

....

....

The most difficult thing is the decision to act, the rest is merely tenacity. Amelia Earhart

Date: / / | I'm Feeling:

I release:

....
....
....

Today's healing:

....
....

I'm grateful for:

....
....
....

I'm inspired by:

....
....

What I give out that I wish to attract today:

....
....
....

Dreams/Notes:

....
....
....
....

The difference between successful people and others is how long they spend time feeling sorry for themselves. Barbara Corcoran

Date: /   /   I'm Feeling:

I release:
....
....
....

Today's healing:
....
....

I'm grateful for:
....
....
....

I'm inspired by:
....
....

What I give out that I wish to attract today:
....
....
....

Dreams/Notes:
....
....
....
....

You can waste your lives drawing lines. Or you can live your life crossing them.
Shonda Rhimes

Date: /   /   I'm Feeling:

I release:

....

....

....

Today's healing:

....

....

I'm grateful for:

....

....

....

I'm inspired by:

....

....

What I give out that I wish to attract today:

....

....

....

Dreams/Notes:

....

....

....

....

I'd rather regret the things I've done than regret the things I haven't done.
Lucille Ball

Date: /   /   I'm Feeling:

I release:
....
....
....

Today's healing:
....
....

I'm grateful for:
....
....
....

I'm inspired by:
....
....

What I give out that I wish to attract today:
....
....
....

Dreams/Notes:
....
....
....
....

Understand that pain pushes us until vision pulls. Michael Beckwith. Clearly visualise and lean into the person and life you want, start vibrating at that higher frequency activated by love, forgiveness, acceptance & gratitude; begin asking what can I give rather than what can I get from the world. You & your life resonate in a way that draws in and attracts what you are.

| Date: / / | I'm Feeling: |

I release:

....

....

....

Today's healing:

....

....

I'm grateful for:

....

....

....

I'm inspired by:

....

....

What I give out that I wish to attract today:

....

....

....

Dreams/Notes:

....

....

....

....

Abundance doesn't start out there– it's a mindset within that's prepared to act generously and with respect toward others and self. This lifts your vibration so the energy of generosity and abundance cannot help but flow back to you. Your thoughts are a magnet that attract what they emit; so wherever possible take a positive approach, avoid gossip and seek to appreciate others. Become what you want to receive. As simple and as hard as that! The Author

Date: / /   I'm Feeling:

I release:

....

....

....

Today's healing:

....

....

I'm grateful for:

....

....

....

I'm inspired by:

....

....

What I give out that I wish to attract today:

....

....

....

Dreams/Notes:

....

....

....

The incredible thing about feeling like you've hit rock bottom and life has no purpose or point, is often the very point we realise the only direction is UP! A new opportunity to start fresh, to build up from stronger foundations, to turn a new page and write a different and better story. The Author

Date: /   /   I'm Feeling:

I release:
....
....
....
....

Today's healing:
....
....
....

I'm grateful for:
....
....
....
....

I'm inspired by:
....
....
....

What I give out that I wish to attract today:
....
....
....
....

Dreams/Notes:
....
....
....
....
....

I have stood on a mountain of No's for one Yes. B. Smith

Date: / /	I'm Feeling:

I release:

....

....

....

Today's healing:

....

....

I'm grateful for:

....

....

....

I'm inspired by:

....

....

What I give out that I wish to attract today:

....

....

....

Dreams/Notes:

....

....

....

....

....

What you do makes a difference, and you have to decide what kind of difference you want to make. Jane Goodall

Date: /   /   I'm Feeling:

I release:
....
....
....

Today's healing:
....
....

I'm grateful for:
....
....
....

I'm inspired by:
....
....

What I give out that I wish to attract today:
....
....
....

Dreams/Notes:
....
....
....
....

If you don't like the road you're walking, start paving another one. Dolly Parton

Date: /   /   I'm Feeling:

I release:

....

....

....

Today's healing:

....

....

I'm grateful for:

....

....

....

I'm inspired by:

....

....

What I give out that I wish to attract today:

....

....

....

Dreams/Notes:

....

....

....

....

The challenge is not to be perfect...it's to be whole. Jane Fonda

Date: /   /

I'm Feeling:

I release:

....

....

....

Today's healing:

....

....

I'm grateful for:

....

....

....

I'm inspired by:

....

....

What I give out that I wish to attract today:

....

....

....

Dreams/Notes:

....

....

....

....

No matter how difficult and painful it may be, nothing sounds as good to the soul as the truth. Martha Beck

Date: / /   I'm Feeling:

I release:

....

....

....

Today's healing:

....

....

I'm grateful for:

....

....

....

I'm inspired by:

....

....

What I give out that I wish to attract today:

....

....

....

Dreams/Notes:

....

....

....

....

When you're through changing, you're through. Martha Stewart

Date: /   /   I'm Feeling:

I release:

....

....

....

Today's healing:

....

....

I'm grateful for:

....

....

....

I'm inspired by:

....

....

What I give out that I wish to attract today:

....

....

....

Dreams/Notes:

....

....

....

Resistance to change creates sorrow and stagnation. It is the nature of life to change and it is our challenge to accept, adapt and allow the changes. Rather than stubbornly looking through the same doorway with the same view, I choose to peer around different doorways and step into new opportunities in my life. I allow reality to be what it is and flow with the tides of change. When I let go of resistance I ease forward into my future. My acceptance brings renewal and clarity. The Author

Date: /   /   I'm Feeling:

I release:

....
....
....

Today's healing:

....
....
....

I'm grateful for:

....
....
....

I'm inspired by:

....
....
....

What I give out that I wish to attract today:

....
....
....

Dreams/Notes:

....
....
....
....

Style is a way to say who you are without having to speak. Rachel Zoe

Date: /   /   I'm Feeling:

I release:
....
....
....

Today's healing:
....
....

I'm grateful for:
....
....
....

I'm inspired by:
....
....

What I give out that I wish to attract today:
....
....
....

Dreams/Notes:
....
....
....
....

Whenever you are blue or lonely or stricken by some humiliating thing you did,
the cure and the hope is in caring about other people. Diane Sawyer

Date: / /	I'm Feeling:

I release:

....

....

....

Today's healing:

....

....

I'm grateful for:

....

....

....

I'm inspired by:

....

....

What I give out that I wish to attract today:

....

....

....

Dreams/Notes:

....

....

....

....

I need to listen well so that I hear what is not said. Thuli Madonsela

Date: /   /   I'm Feeling:

I release:
....
....
....

Today's healing:
....
....

I'm grateful for:
....
....
....

I'm inspired by:
....
....

What I give out that I wish to attract today:
....
....
....

Dreams/Notes:
....
....
....

If you have been avoiding a task that feels like Mt Everest and you don't know where to start: chunk it down into small, manageable milestones and take one simple step towards your goal. A huge tree begins as a seed, a vast building begins with one brick and the journey of a thousand miles starts with just one step. The Author

Date: /   /   I'm Feeling:

I release:
....
....
....

Today's healing:
....
....

I'm grateful for:
....
....
....

I'm inspired by:
....
....

What I give out that I wish to attract today:
....
....
....

Dreams/Notes:
....
....
....

Remembering to play and have fun is essential to balance and as a counter to life's seriousness. Play and laughter lighten the heart, release our natural pharmacy of endorphins, improve circulation, lessen anger and resentment and act as medicine for the heart. The Author

100

Date: /   /   I'm Feeling:

I release:
....
....
....

Today's healing:
....
....

I'm grateful for:
....
....
....

I'm inspired by:
....
....

What I give out that I wish to attract today:
....
....
....

Dreams/Notes:
....
....
....
....

Step out of the history that is holding you back. Step into the new story you are willing to create. Oprah Winfrey

Date: / /   I'm Feeling:

I release:

....

....

....

Today's healing:

....

....

I'm grateful for:

....

....

....

I'm inspired by:

....

....

What I give out that I wish to attract today:

....

....

....

Dreams/Notes:

....

....

....

....

....

I try to live in a little bit of my own joy and not let people steal it or take it. Hoda Kotb

Date: /   /   I'm Feeling:

I release:
....
....
....

Today's healing:
....
....

I'm grateful for:
....
....
....

I'm inspired by:
....
....

What I give out that I wish to attract today:
....
....
....

Dreams/Notes:
....
....
....
....

If you obey all the rules, you miss all the fun. Katharine Hepburn

Date: / /	I'm Feeling:

I release:

....
....
....

Today's healing:

....
....

I'm grateful for:

....
....
....

I'm inspired by:

....
....

What I give out that I wish to attract today:

....
....
....

Dreams/Notes:

....
....
....
....

Being deeply loved by someone gives you strength, while loving someone deeply gives you courage. Lao Tzu

Date: /   /   I'm Feeling:

I release:
....
....
....

Today's healing:
....
....

I'm grateful for:
....
....
....

I'm inspired by:
....
....

What I give out that I wish to attract today:
....
....
....

Dreams/Notes:
....
....
....
....

Many receive advice, only the wise profit from it. Harper Lee

Date: /   /   I'm Feeling:

I release:

Today's healing:

I'm grateful for:

I'm inspired by:

What I give out that I wish to attract today:

Dreams/Notes:

One of the secrets to staying young is to always do things you don't know how to do, to keep learning. Ruth Reichl

Date: /   /   I'm Feeling:

I release:
....
....
....

Today's healing:
....
....

I'm grateful for:
....
....
....

I'm inspired by:
....
....

What I give out that I wish to attract today:
....
....
....

Dreams/Notes:
....
....
....
....

It took me quite a long time to develop a voice, and now that I have it, I am not going to be silent. Madeleine Albright

Date: /   /   I'm Feeling:

I release:

....

....

Today's healing:

....

I'm grateful for:

....

....

I'm inspired by:

....

....

What I give out that I wish to attract today:

....

....

Dreams/Notes:

....

....

....

....

Learn from the mistakes of others. You can't live long enough to make them all yourself. Eleanor Roosevelt

Date: / / | I'm Feeling:

I release:
....
....
....

Today's healing:
....
....

I'm grateful for:
....
....
....

I'm inspired by:
....
....

What I give out that I wish to attract today:
....
....
....

Dreams/Notes:
....
....
....
....

To love and be loved is to feel the sun from both sides. David Viscott

Date: /   /   I'm Feeling:

I release:
....
....
....

Today's healing:
....
....

I'm grateful for:
....
....
....

I'm inspired by:
....
....

What I give out that I wish to attract today:
....
....
....

Dreams/Notes:
....
....
....
....
....

The best thing to hold onto in life is each other. Audrey Hepburn

Date: / /	I'm Feeling:

I release:

....

....

....

Today's healing:

....

....

I'm grateful for:

....

....

....

I'm inspired by:

....

....

What I give out that I wish to attract today:

....

....

....

Dreams/Notes:

....

....

....

Wise Life Advice Part I: 1) Let it go; why ruin a good today by thinking of a bad yesterday? 2) Ignore them; they have a right to their opinion but you don't have to agree with it– live life on your terms 3) Give it Time; time heals everything, including a broken heart.

Date: /   /   I'm Feeling:

I release:

....

....

....

Today's healing:

....

....

....

I'm grateful for:

....

....

....

I'm inspired by:

....

....

....

What I give out that I wish to attract today:

....

....

....

....

Dreams/Notes:

....

....

....

....

Wise Life Advice Part II: 4) Don't Compare; the only person to beat is the person you were yesterday 5) Stay Calm; you don't have to have everything figured out right now 6) It's on you; you get to choose how to respond and be content in any given situation 7) Smile; life is short and precious.

Date: /   /

I'm Feeling:

I release:

....
....
....

Today's healing:

....
....

I'm grateful for:

....
....
....

I'm inspired by:

....
....

What I give out that I wish to attract today:

....
....
....

Dreams/Notes:

....
....
....
....
....

Normal is not something to aspire to, it's something to get away from. Jodie Foster

Date: /   /   I'm Feeling:

I release:

....

....

....

Today's healing:

....

....

I'm grateful for:

....

....

....

I'm inspired by:

....

....

What I give out that I wish to attract today:

....

....

....

Dreams/Notes:

....

....

....

....

I learned a long time ago that there is something worse than missing the goal, and that's not pulling the trigger. Mia Hamm

Date: / /   I'm Feeling:

I release:

....
....
....
....

Today's healing:

....
....

I'm grateful for:

....
....
....
....

I'm inspired by:

....
....

What I give out that I wish to attract today:

....
....
....
....

Dreams/Notes:

....
....
....
....
....

Owning our story can be hard but not nearly as difficult as spending our lives running from it. Brené Brown

Date: /   / | I'm Feeling:

I release:
....
....
....

Today's healing:
....
....

I'm grateful for:
....
....
....

I'm inspired by:
....
....

What I give out that I wish to attract today:
....
....
....

Dreams/Notes:
....
....
....
....

I do not try to dance better than anyone else. I only try to dance better than myself. Arianna Huffington

Date: /   / | I'm Feeling:

I release:

....
....
....

Today's healing:

....
....

I'm grateful for:

....
....
....

I'm inspired by:

....
....

What I give out that I wish to attract today:

....
....
....

Dreams/Notes:

....
....
....
....

In order to be irreplaceable one must always be different. Coco Chanel

Date: /   /   I'm Feeling:

I release:
....
....
....

Today's healing:
....
....

I'm grateful for:
....
....

I'm inspired by:
....
....

What I give out that I wish to attract today:
....
....
....

Dreams/Notes:
....
....
....
....

If you can't go straight ahead, you go around the corner. Cher

Date: /   / | I'm Feeling:

I release:

....
....
....

Today's healing:

....
....

I'm grateful for:

....
....
....

I'm inspired by:

....
....

What I give out that I wish to attract today:

....
....
....

Dreams/Notes:

....
....
....
....

If you don't get out of the box you've been raised in, you won't understand how much bigger the world is. Angelina Jolie

Date: / /   I'm Feeling:

I release:

....
....
....

Today's healing:

....
....

I'm grateful for:

....
....
....

I'm inspired by:

....
....

What I give out that I wish to attract today:

....
....
....

Dreams/Notes:

....
....
....
....
....

If you're someone people count on, particularly in difficult moments, that's a sign of a life lived honorably. Rachel Maddow

Date: /   /   I'm Feeling:

I release:

....

....

....

Today's healing:

....

....

I'm grateful for:

....

....

....

I'm inspired by:

....

....

What I give out that I wish to attract today:

....

....

....

Dreams/Notes:

....

....

....

....

You can't be that kid standing at the top of the water slide, overthinking it. You have to go down the chute. Tina Fey

Date: /   /   I'm Feeling:

I release:

....

....

....

Today's healing:

....

....

I'm grateful for:

....

....

....

I'm inspired by:

....

....

What I give out that I wish to attract today:

....

....

....

Dreams/Notes:

....

....

....

....

There are two kinds of people, those who do the work and those who take the credit. Try to be in the first group; there is less competition there. Indira Gandhi

Date: / / | I'm Feeling:

I release:

....
....
....
....

Today's healing:

....
....
....

I'm grateful for:

....
....
....
....

I'm inspired by:

....
....
....

What I give out that I wish to attract today:

....
....
....

Dreams/Notes:

....
....
....
....
....

All careers go up and down like friendships, like marriages, like anything else, and you can't bat a thousand all the time. Julie Andrews

Date: /   / | I'm Feeling:

I release:

....

....

....

Today's healing:

....

....

I'm grateful for:

....

....

....

I'm inspired by:

....

....

What I give out that I wish to attract today:

....

....

....

Dreams/Notes:

....

....

....

....

....

I grow where I'm planted. I'm a unique expression of the Infinite and on my own unique journey of unfolding and growing. I ask who and what I am, what is my purpose and live into my best expression of that. Michael Beckwith

Date: / /	I'm Feeling:

I release:

....

....

....

Today's healing:

....

....

I'm grateful for:

....

....

....

I'm inspired by:

....

....

What I give out that I wish to attract today:

....

....

....

Dreams/Notes:

....

....

....

....

A strong woman is a woman determined to do something others are determined not be done. Marge Piercy

Date: /   /   I'm Feeling:

I release:
....
....
....

Today's healing:
....
....

I'm grateful for:
....
....
....

I'm inspired by:
....
....

What I give out that I wish to attract today:
....
....
....

Dreams/Notes:
....
....
....
....
....

The question isn't who's going to let me; it's who is going to stop me. Ayn Rand

Date: /   / | I'm Feeling:

I release:

....
....
....

Today's healing:

....
....

I'm grateful for:

....
....
....

I'm inspired by:

....
....

What I give out that I wish to attract today:

....
....
....

Dreams/Notes:

....
....
....
....

I choose to make the rest of my life the best of my life. Louise Hay

Date: / /	I'm Feeling:

I release:

....

....

....

Today's healing:

....

....

I'm grateful for:

....

....

....

I'm inspired by:

....

....

What I give out that I wish to attract today:

....

....

....

Dreams/Notes:

....

....

....

....

When you're sick and tired of being sick and tired ask for H.E.L.P. Say Hello Eternal Loving Presence, I'm open and available to something new now! Michael Beckwith

Date: / /

I'm Feeling:

I release:

....
....
....

Today's healing:

....
....

I'm grateful for:

....
....
....

I'm inspired by:

....
....

What I give out that I wish to attract today:

....
....
....

Dreams/Notes:

....
....
....
....

Spread love everywhere you go. Let no one ever come to you without leaving happier. Mother Theresa

Date: /   /   I'm Feeling:

I release:

....

....

....

Today's healing:

....

....

I'm grateful for:

....

....

....

I'm inspired by:

....

....

What I give out that I wish to attract today:

....

....

....

Dreams/Notes:

....

....

....

....

When we speak we are afraid our words will not be heard or welcomed. But when we are silent, we are still afraid. So it is better to speak. Audre Lorde

Date: /   /   I'm Feeling:

I release:

....
....
....

Today's healing:

....
....

I'm grateful for:

....
....
....

I'm inspired by:

....
....

What I give out that I wish to attract today:

....
....
....

Dreams/Notes:

....
....
....
....

Above all, be the heroine of your life, not the victim. Nora Ephron

Date: /   /   I'm Feeling:

I release:

....

....

....

Today's healing:

....

....

....

I'm grateful for:

....

....

....

I'm inspired by:

....

....

....

What I give out that I wish to attract today:

....

....

....

Dreams/Notes:

....

....

....

....

Change your life today. Don't gamble on the future, act now, without delay.
Simone de Beauvoir

Date: /   / | I'm Feeling:

I release:

....

....

....

Today's healing:

....

....

I'm grateful for:

....

....

....

I'm inspired by:

....

....

What I give out that I wish to attract today:

....

....

....

Dreams/Notes:

....

....

....

....

The most common way people give up their power is by thinking they don't have any. Alice Walker

Date: /   /

I'm Feeling:

I release:

....

....

....

Today's healing:

....

....

I'm grateful for:

....

....

....

I'm inspired by:

....

....

What I give out that I wish to attract today:

....

....

....

Dreams/Notes:

....

....

....

....

Doubt is a killer. You just have to know who you are and what you stand for.
Jennifer Lopez

Date: /   /   I'm Feeling:

I release:
....
....
....

Today's healing:
....
....

I'm grateful for:
....
....
....

I'm inspired by:
....
....

What I give out that I wish to attract today:
....
....
....

Dreams/Notes:
....
....
....

If what we resist persists then look at all the things that you resist and all the ways that you have kept yourself stuck. Once the urge to expand, discover and grow becomes more powerful than the burden of resisting for fear of change: its game over. The Author

Date: /   /   I'm Feeling:

I release:

....

....

....

Today's healing:

....

....

I'm grateful for:

....

....

....

I'm inspired by:

....

....

What I give out that I wish to attract today:

....

....

....

Dreams/Notes:

....

....

....

....

Life is not measured by the number of breaths we take, but the moments that take our breath away. Maya Angelou

Date: /   /   I'm Feeling:

I release:
....
....
....

Today's healing:
....
....

I'm grateful for:
....
....
....

I'm inspired by:
....
....

What I give out that I wish to attract today:
....
....
....

Dreams/Notes:
....
....
....
....

If you don't like being a doormat then get off the floor. Al Anon

Date: / /   I'm Feeling:

I release:

....

....

Today's healing:

....

....

I'm grateful for:

....

....

I'm inspired by:

....

....

What I give out that I wish to attract today:

....

....

....

Dreams/Notes:

....

....

....

....

Whatever you do, be different – that was the advice my mother gave me, and I can't think of better advice for an entrepreneur. If you're different, you will stand out. Anita Roddick

Date: / /	I'm Feeling:

I release:

....

....

....

Today's healing:

....

....

I'm grateful for:

....

....

....

I'm inspired by:

....

....

What I give out that I wish to attract today:

....

....

....

Dreams/Notes:

....

....

....

....

A lot of people are afraid to say what they want. That's why they don't get what they want. Madonna

Date: /   /   I'm Feeling:

I release:

....
....
....

Today's healing:

....
....

I'm grateful for:

....
....
....

I'm inspired by:

....
....

What I give out that I wish to attract today:

....
....
....

Dreams/Notes:

....
....
....
....

Your task is not to seek for love, but merely to seek and find all the barriers within yourself that you have built against it. Rumi

Date: /   /   I'm Feeling:

I release:
....
....
....

Today's healing:
....
....

I'm grateful for:
....
....
....

I'm inspired by:
....
....

What I give out that I wish to attract today:
....
....
....

Dreams/Notes:
....
....
....
....
....

A strong woman understands that gifts such as logic, decisiveness, and strength are just as feminine as intuition and emotional connection. She values and uses all of her gifts. Nancy Rathburn